2ND EDITION

PIANO

LEVEL **1**

P9-DNT-687

Adventures® *by Nancy and Randall Faber*

THE BASIC PIANO METHOD

This book belongs to: _Srisha vishwanath ♡☆♡ ♡☆♡_

Montclair Music Studio
104 Watchung Avenue
Upper Montclair, NJ 07043
973-783-4330

Thanks and acknowledgement to Victoria McArthur
for her collaboration on the First Edition of this book.

FABER
PIANO ADVENTURES®
3042 Creek Drive
Ann Arbor, Michigan 48108

The Slur

Legato means to play smoothly, connecting the notes.

A **slur** is a curved line placed by the noteheads (not the stem). It means to play legato.

slur

slur

Legato River Melody

1. • Draw a **slur** from the *first* note to the *last* note for each line.

• Notice the time signature. Add a bar line after every **4 beats**.

• Draw a "smiley face" above each measure with the
same melody as *measure 1*.

Smooth and flowing

2. Now play the music on the piano.
After playing, your teacher may ask you to write the **note names** beside each note.

QUESTION: How are a melody and a river alike?

ANSWER: They both twist and turn. Neither go in a straight line!

Sailing Melodies

1. Connect each melody to the "river" that matches its shape.
Hint: It may help you to play the music first.

e. Can YOU draw the shape for this melody?

Sailing Slurs

2. Now draw a **slur** from the *first note* to the *last note* for each melody above.
Play and listen for a smooth, legato sound.

Lesson p.11 (Sailing in the Sun)

To **improvise** means to create "on the spot."

Ferris Wheel Improv

Improvise ferris wheel music by doing the following:

1. First, listen to your teacher play the accompaniment.
Feel the "round-and-round" turning rhythm.

2. When you are ready, play notes from a high **C 5-finger scale** IN ANY ORDER.
Hint: Create short **legato** melodies that use steps and skips.

3. When your teacher stops and holds, you do the same. The ferris wheel has stopped to let someone off. Then start it up again!

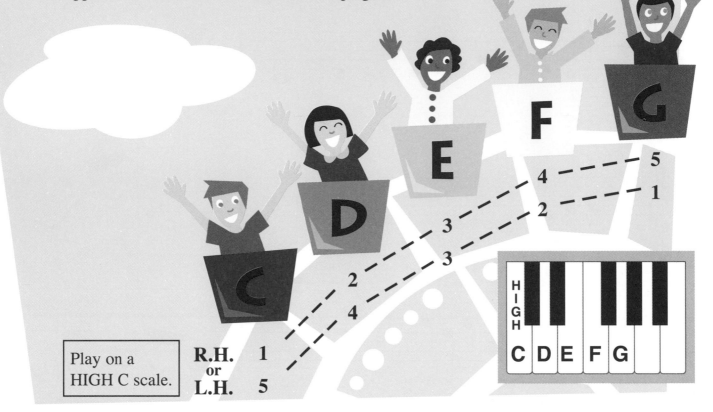

Play on a HIGH C scale.

R.H. 1
or
L.H. 5

Teacher Improv Accompaniment and "Story"

"Hold. We're letting someone off! Now start the ferris wheel again."

"It's stopping again to let someone else off," etc.

Repeat ad lib.

Ending

rit.

8va

More Improv Ideas
- Take the riders to the very top and hold.
- Bring them back down!
- Student holds a C to end.

A **slur** curves over or under a group of notes.

A **tie** connects one note to the very *same* note.

Write **slur** or **tie** under each example.

Ex. _slur_

Slur

Tie

Slur

Slur

Tie

Listen: Your teacher will play a group of notes.

- Do you hear **steps** or **skips**? (*circle*)
- Was it *forte* or *piano*? (*circle*)

steps or skips

steps or skips

steps or skips

steps or skips

f or *p*

f or *p*

f or *p*

f or *p*

For Teacher Use Only: The examples may be played in any order. Ask students to close their eyes as you play.

Playing Staccato

 or

The **staccato mark** is a dot above or below the notehead.

Staccato means to let go of the key quickly for a crisp, separated sound. Think of jumping beans!

Staccato is the opposite of **legato**.

What Is Jumping on the Rug?

1. Complete the following:

    • Draw a staccato dot for each note.

    • Draw bar lines after every **4 beats**.

2. Play the song and let your fingers hop!

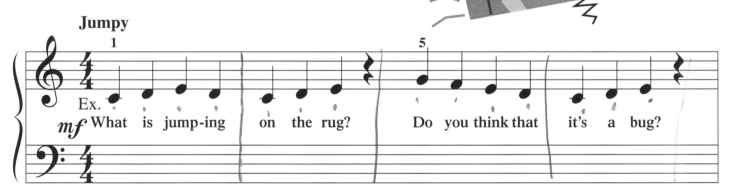

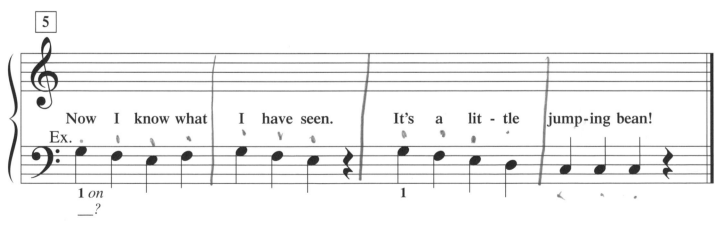

3. Now play the song completely **legato**. Give it a new title:

    Snaily

    MY TITLE

For staccato notes, the dot is placed **above** or **below** the notehead.

For dotted half notes, the dot is placed **beside** the half note.

The Dotted Mouse in the Haunted House

1. Circle each **staccato** note.
   Hint: There are 10.

2. Draw a triangle around each **dotted half note**.
   Hint: There are 10.

Lesson p.15 (The Haunted Mouse)

Remember, to **improvise** means to create "on the spot."

Improvise young hunter music by doing the following:

1. First, listen to your teacher play the accompaniment.
   Say "legato" or "staccato" as you hear the music change.

2. When you are ready, use these 5 white keys IN ANY ORDER.
   When the teacher part is **legato**, can you play *legato* to match?
   When the teacher part is **staccato**, can you play *staccato* to match?

Young Hunter Improv

Play HIGH on the keyboard.

R.H. or L.H.

Teacher Improv Accompaniment

Lesson p.17 (Young Hunter)

Step and Skip Hunt

Write **step** or **skip** under each example.

Your teacher may ask you to write the note names above each example.

Ex. __skip__   _Step_   _skip_   _step_

skip   _step_   _skip_   _step_

Your teacher will play a musical example.

- If you hear only *staccato* sounds, circle the box with only **staccato dots**.

- If you hear only *legato* sounds, circle the box with a **slur.**

- If you hear both *staccato* and *legato*, circle the box with **staccato dots** and a **slur.**

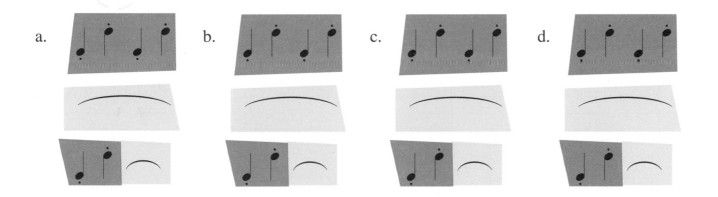

a.   b.   c.   d.

For Teacher Use Only: The examples may be played in any order.

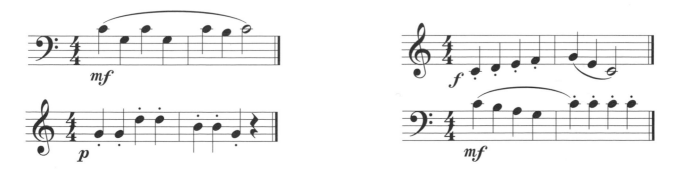

Face the Treble Clef

Memorize: The spaces on the treble staff spell the word

F A C E

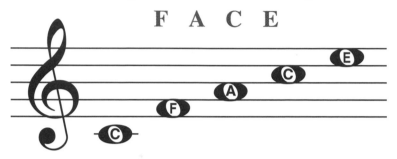

• Say and play F-A-C-E on the keys 4 times.

Planets in Space

1. Cover up the staff above. Write the missing space letter names to complete the "planets."

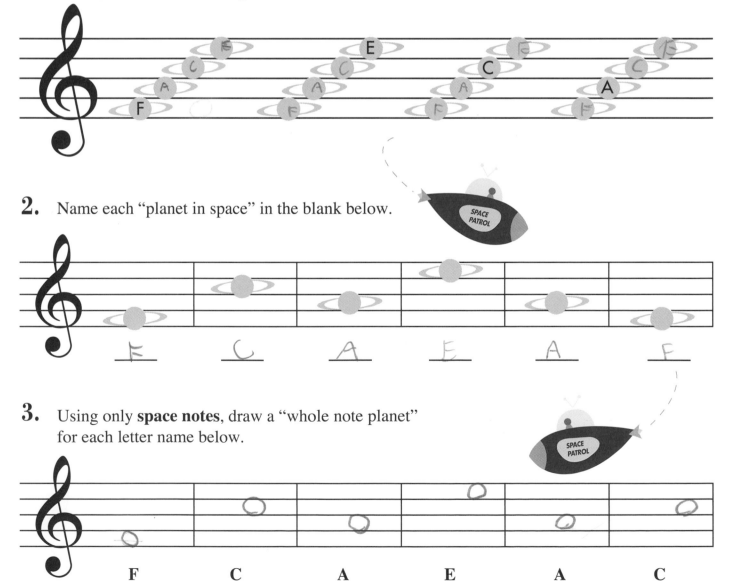

2. Name each "planet in space" in the blank below.

3. Using only **space notes**, draw a "whole note planet" for each letter name below.

F   C   A   E   A   C

You Complete the Music!

Complete the music by doing the following:

- Draw measure bars to match the **time signature**.
- Draw *staccato* dots for each note in LINE 2.
- Write the letter names beside (or under) every note.
- Play *Rah Rah Cheer!*

Rah Rah Cheer!

With energy

Ex. F   A   F   A   F A C A   F A C
f Rah,   rah,   rah,   rah,   cheer for our team   on the field!

5 (Draw *staccato* dots for this line of music.)

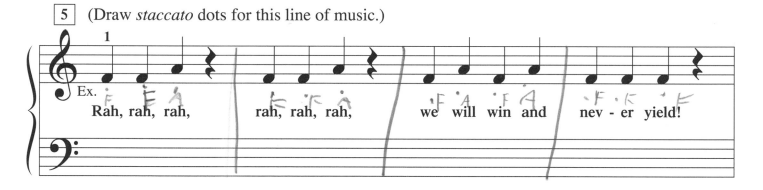

Ex. F F A   F F A   F A F A   F F F
Rah, rah, rah,   rah, rah, rah,   we will win and   nev - er yield!

9

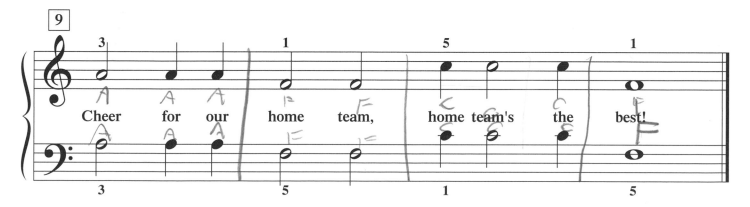

A   A   A   F   F   C   C   F
Cheer   for   our   home   team,   home team's   the   best!
A   A   A   F   F

Can you transpose *Rah Rah Cheer!* to **C** and **G 5-finger scales**?

Sightreading — to play a piece for the first time.

After reading the hints below, **sightread** *Forest Dance*.

- First, look through each measure. Can you spot **steps** and **skips**?

- Set a slow, steady beat with a "count-off" measure: "1-2-3-4."

- Begin to play. Keep your eyes on the music and don't stop. The forest dance must go on!

Forest Dance

Can you transpose this piece to **C** and **G 5-finger scales**?

Li'l Liza Skips

Your teacher will play the given note and then another note a skip up or skip down.

Listen carefully, then draw a whole note a **skip up** or **down** from the given note. ✏
Think space to space!

Li'l Liza Rhythms

LISTEN!
TAP THE RHYTHM!

- Close your eyes and listen. Your teacher will play a tune on the piano.

- On your lap, tap back the **rhythm** that you hear.

For Teacher Use Only: The tunes may be repeated several times. Optional: Sing the words as you play.

📖 Lesson p.21 (Li'l Liza Jane)

Focus on Middle C and Treble C

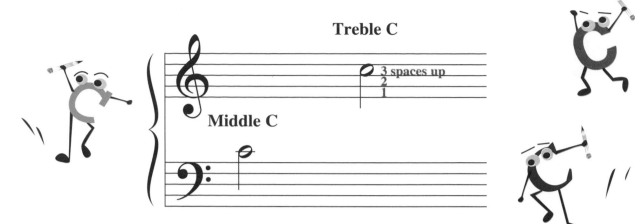

Treble C
3 spaces up
3
2
1

Middle C

1. Draw **Middle C's** or **Treble C's** for each measure.
Use the rhythm given.

Break-Out Boogie

Fast rock beat

3

f Ex.

3

5

2. Now play with the teacher duet. Use braced **finger 3's**.

Teacher Duet: (Student plays *as written*)

Play 4 times! 5   *Play 2 times!*

mf
5 1 4 3 2 1   5 1 4 3 2 1   5   2 1 2

8va lower throughout

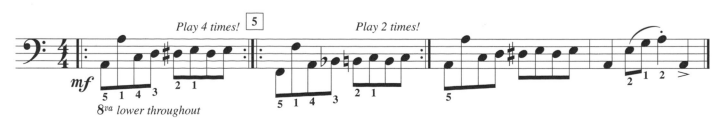

Rules for Stems

Notes **below line 3** have UP stems. Notes **on** or **above line 3** have DOWN stems.

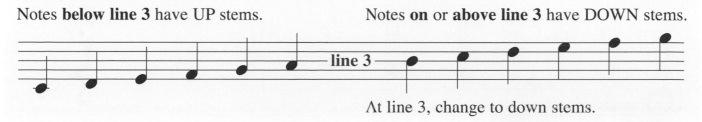

line 3

At line 3, change to down stems.

Mozart's Story

- Draw stems correctly on the noteheads below.

- Name the notes to spell words and then read the story.

Ex.

Mozart lov _e d_   g __ m __ s   and   pr __ __ tical

jok __ s, but was also a   k __ __ n   stu __ __ nt.   By the __ __ __ of six,

he __ oul __ play the violin and   k __ ybo __ r __ .   His __ __ th __ r

took youn __ Mozart on __ r __ n __ tours of Europe to show off his   t __ l __ nt.

The ro __ __ s were bumpy and slow, with __ __ n __ __ rous   b __ n __ its.

Mozart __ r __ ss __ __ as a little __ __ ult and played with a sword at his sid __ !

Treble C-D-E-F-G

Treble C   **D**   **E**   **F**   **G**

space   line   space   line   space

Paper Airplane Flight

- Answer the following for this paper airplane flight.

Draw **Treble C D E F G.**
Use quarter notes as above.

step or skip? *(circle)*

note names ___ ___

step or skip?

note names ___ ___

step or skip? ___ ___

step or skip? ___ ___

step or skip? ___ ___

step or skip? ___ ___

step or skip? ___ ___

step or skip?

SAFE LANDING!

16   Lesson p.24 (Paper Airplane)   FF1079

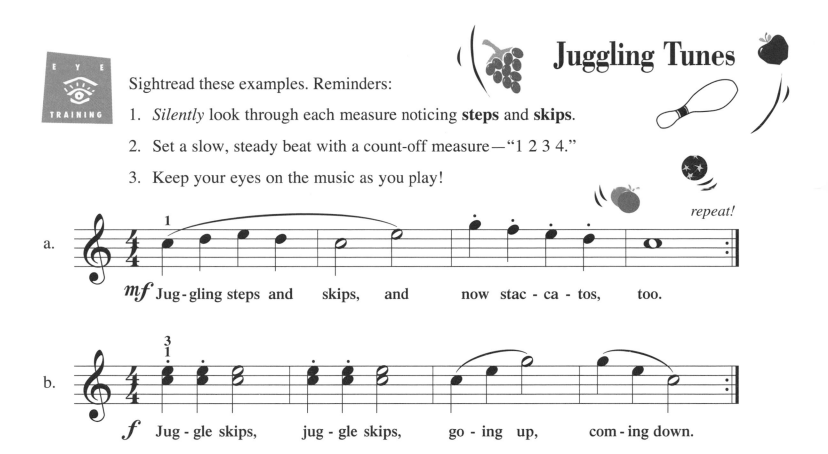

Juggling Tunes

EYE TRAINING

Sightread these examples. Reminders:

1. *Silently* look through each measure noticing **steps** and **skips**.

2. Set a slow, steady beat with a count-off measure—"1 2 3 4."

3. Keep your eyes on the music as you play!

a. *mf* Jug-gling steps and   skips,   and   now stac-ca-tos,   too.

b. *f* Jug-gle skips,   jug-gle skips,   go-ing up,   com-ing down.

EAR TRAINING

Close your eyes. Your teacher will play **Bass C**, **Middle C**, or **Treble C**.
Listen and write the correct C on the staffs below.

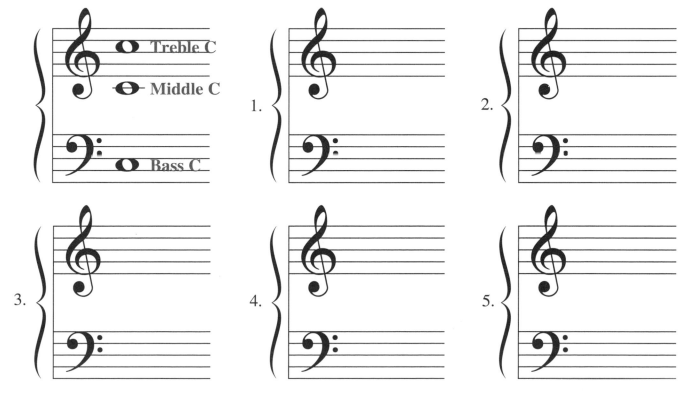

Treble C

Middle C

Bass C

1.

2.

3.

4.

5.

For Teacher Use Only: The examples may be played in any order.

4 UNIT

2nd = Step

Remember, an **interval** is the distance between two notes.

On the Keys

C D

Count: **1   2 = 2nd**

On the Staff

2nd

line to space

or

2nd

space to line

Traffic Jam 2nds!

1. Draw an ✗ a 2nd ABOVE each car. Then name both notes.

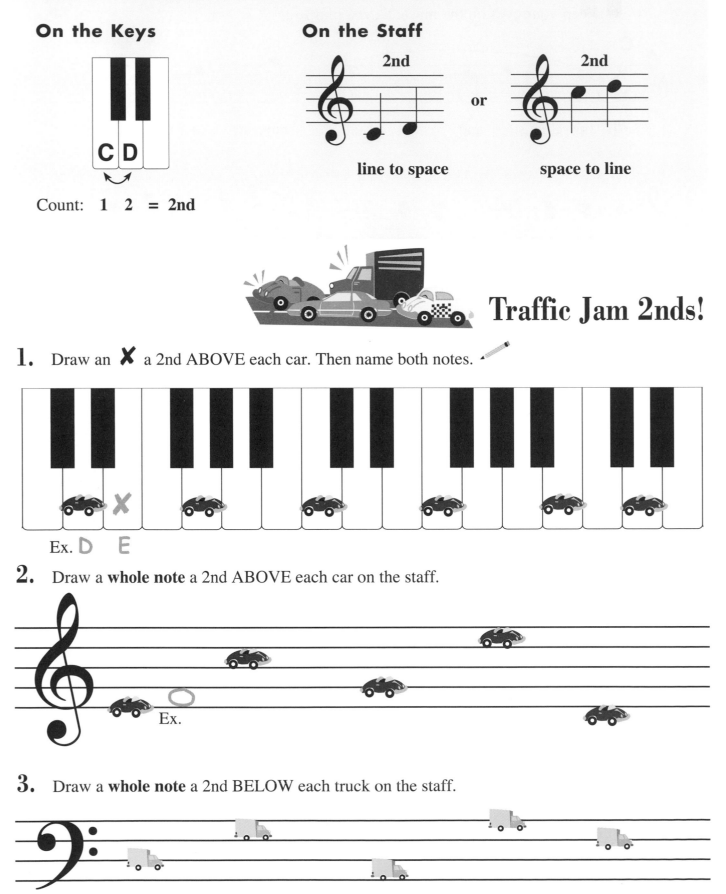

Ex. D E

2. Draw a **whole note** a 2nd ABOVE each car on the staff.

Ex.

3. Draw a **whole note** a 2nd BELOW each truck on the staff.

3rd = Skip

On the Keys

A 3rd spans 3 letter names.

C   E

Count: 1 2 3 = 3rd

On the Staff

3rd

line to line

or

3rd

space to space

EYE TRAINING

Write a big **2** on the kites that use **2nds**. Write a big **3** on the kites that use **3rds**.

• Draw a **3rd higher**.

• Draw a **3rd lower**.

EAR TRAINING

Close your eyes. Your teacher will play a **2nd** or **3rd** (notes separately, then together). Circle the interval you hear.

a. **2nd**   **3rd**   b. **2nd**   **3rd**   c. **2nd**   **3rd**   d. **2nd**   **3rd**

For Teacher Use Only: The examples may be played in any order. Create more examples of your own.

4th = a Skip Plus a Step

On the Keys

On the Staff

4th — line to space — or — 4th — space to line

Count: **1   2   3   4 = 4th**   A 4th spans 4 letters.

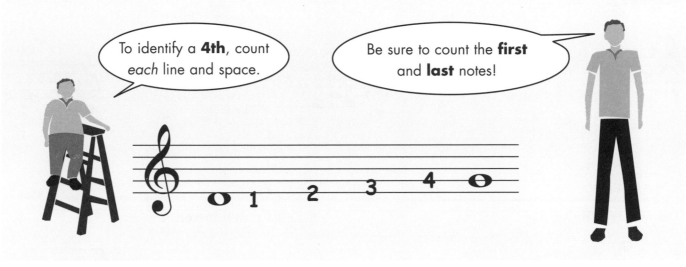

To identify a **4th**, count *each* line and space.

Be sure to count the **first** and **last** notes!

Mixed-Up Intervals

1. Write a **3rd UP**, then a **4th UP** for each example.
   Write the letter names below the notes.

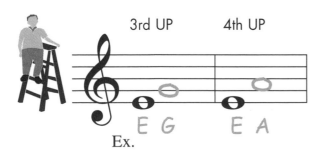

3rd UP   4th UP

E G   E A

Ex.

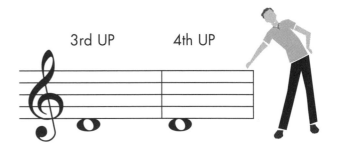

3rd UP   4th UP

3rd UP   4th UP

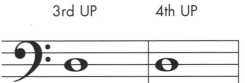

3rd UP   4th UP

2. Write a **3rd DOWN**, then a **4th DOWN** for each example.
Write the letter names below the notes.

Close your eyes. Your teacher will play a **2nd**, **3rd**, or **4th**. Listen for the notes played separately, then together.

Circle the interval you hear.

a. **2nd** **3rd** **4th**   b. **2nd** **3rd** **4th**   c. **2nd** **3rd** **4th**

d. **2nd** **3rd** **4th**   e. **2nd** **3rd** **4th**   f. **2nd** **3rd** **4th**

For Teacher Use Only: The examples may be played in any order and repeated several times.
Create additional intervals (2nd, 3rd, 4th) using this model.

Lesson p.30 (A Mixed-Up Song)

5th = a Skip Plus a Skip

On the Keys

Count: **1 2 3 4 5 = 5th**

On the Staff

5th

or

5th

line to line   **space to space**

A 5th spans 5 letters.

To identify a **5th**, count each line and space.
Be sure to count the **first** and **last** notes!

Sounds from the Rain Forest

1. Write a **3rd UP**, then a **5th UP** for each sound from the rain forest.
    Your teacher may ask you to write the letter names below the notes.

3rd ↑   5th ↑

Ex. E G   E B

Hint: Think
skip plus a skip.

3rd ↑   5th ↑

…the toucan's call

3rd ↑   5th ↑

…the lion's roar

3rd ↑   5th ↑

…the parrot squawking

... and More Sounds (2nds, 3rds, 4ths, 5ths)

2. Now draw **2nds**, **3rds**, **4ths**, or **5ths** for each example below. ✏️
The arrows tell you UP or DOWN.

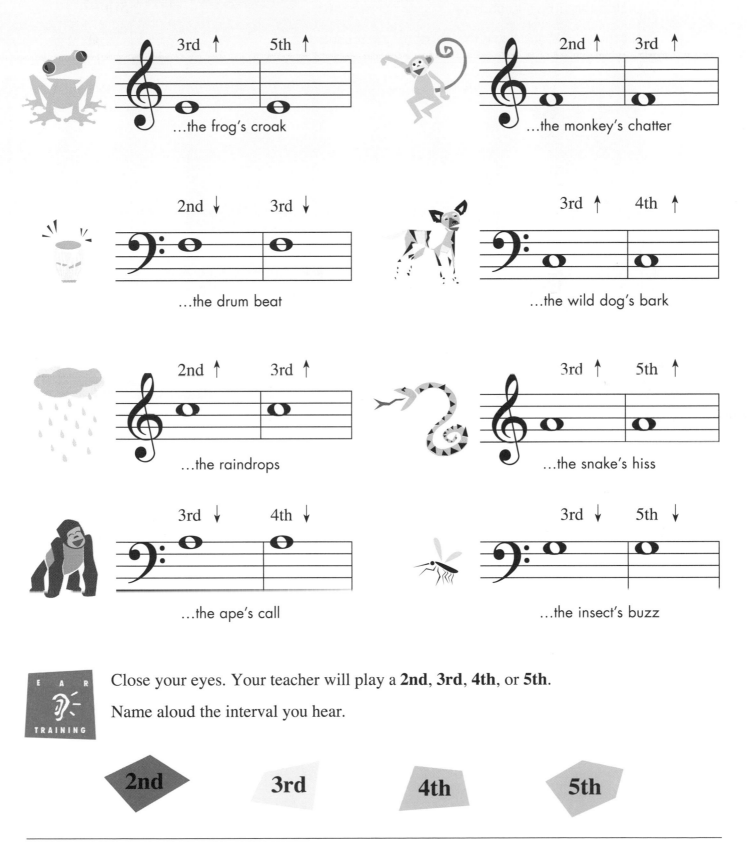

...the frog's croak

...the monkey's chatter

...the drum beat

...the wild dog's bark

...the raindrops

...the snake's hiss

...the ape's call

...the insect's buzz

EAR TRAINING Close your eyes. Your teacher will play a **2nd**, **3rd**, **4th**, or **5th**.

Name aloud the interval you hear.

2nd **3rd** **4th** **5th**

For Teacher Use Only: The examples may be played in any order and repeated several times.
Create additional intervals (2nd, 3rd, 4th, 5th) using this model.

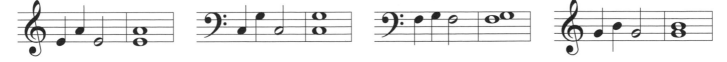

Lightly Snow

1. Complete the snowman by doing the following:

   - Turn your book to the side and draw **bar lines** to match the time signature.

   - Read the words and trace the **slurs** for each hand.

2. Ask your teacher to hold the book for you and play *Lightly Snow* hands together!

Lesson p.35 (Lightly Row)

Draw a
Double Bar Line.
(thin line, thick line)

FF1079

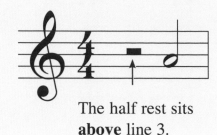

Half Rest

2 beats of silence

The half rest sits
above line 3.

Whole Rest

**4 beats of silence, or rest
for any *whole* measure**

The whole rest hangs
below line 4.

Forest Drum Rhythms

Your teacher will depress the damper pedal.

1. With your teacher, use your palms to tap the rhythm
on the wood underneath the keyboard. Listen to the
interesting sound!

2. Now tap the rhythm while your teacher plays the duet.

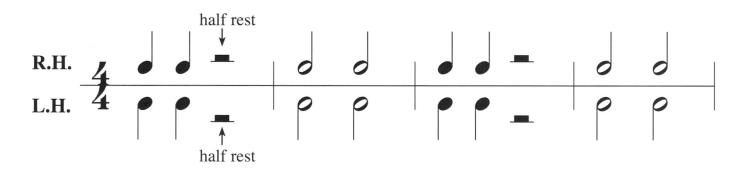

R.H.

L.H.

half rest

half rest

Teacher Duet: (Student taps on a drum or on the wood underneath the keyboard)

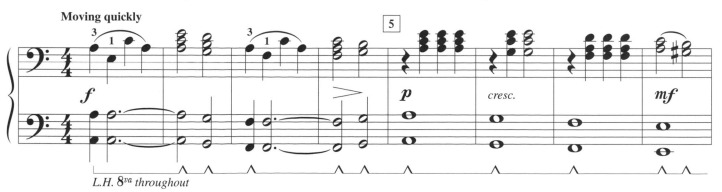

Moving quickly

f

p

cresc.

mf

L.H. 8va throughout

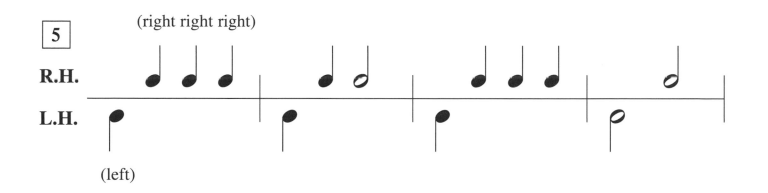

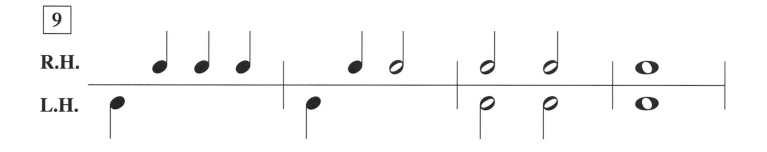

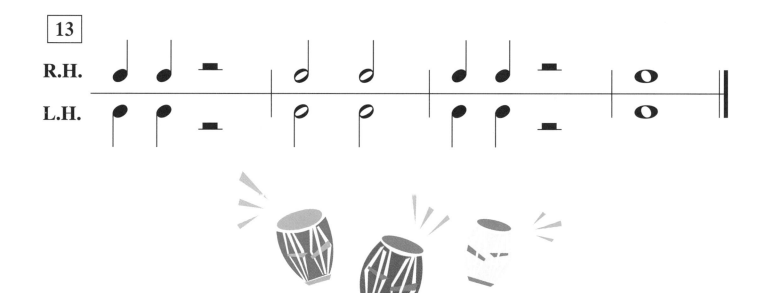

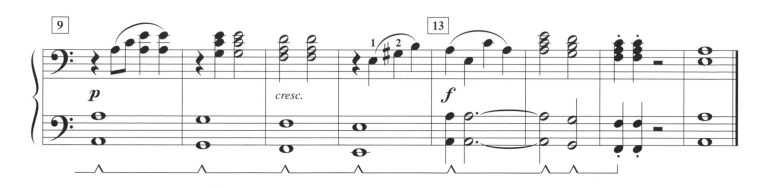

Drawing Rests

1. Draw a **half rest** in each measure for the R.H.

2. Draw a **whole rest** in each measure for the L.H.
   Then play this melody that "climbs up" to the moon.

Climbing to the Moon

Gently

half rest sits on line 3

draw

Climb-ing, *half rest,* climb-ing, *half rest,* climb-ing, *half rest,* climb-ing, *half rest,*

whole rest hangs below line 4

draw

5
climb - ing, *half rest,* climb - ing, *half rest,* climb - ing, *half rest,* high!

3. Draw *one* rest to complete each measure.   quarter rest 𝄽   half rest ▬   whole rest ▬

Ex.

Notice the **time signature**!

Grumpy Old Rests

Grumpy Old Troll has made mistakes on his theory work below.

- Put an X through the measures with **too many beats**.

- Put an X through the measures with **too few beats**.

Your teacher will set a steady beat for you to tap with your hand or foot.

- As you tap, listen to the musical example that your teacher plays.
- Circle the kind of rest you hear in each example.

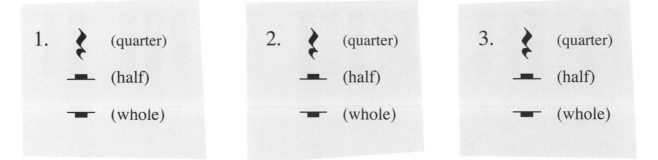

1. 𝄽 (quarter)
▬ (half)
▬ (whole)

2. 𝄽 (quarter)
▬ (half)
▬ (whole)

3. 𝄽 (quarter)
▬ (half)
▬ (whole)

For Teacher Use Only: The examples may be played in any order. Set a steady beat for the student to tap as you play. Count one measure aloud before each example.

📖 Lesson p.39 (Grumpy Old Troll)

The Sharp ♯

A *sharp* means to play the key a **half step higher** (the closest key to the right).

Merlin's Sharps

1. Trace these sharps. ✏️   ♯ ♯ ♯ ♯

Now draw your own ♯ in each of Merlin's stars.

2. Connect the **sharp letter name** in Merlin's wands to the correct key.

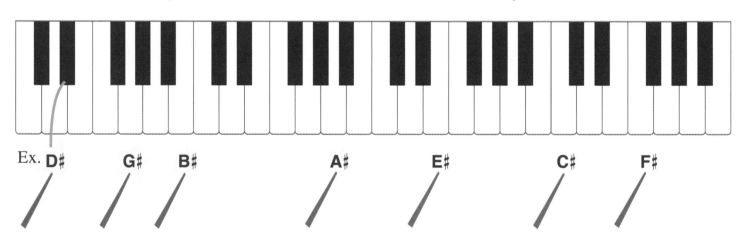

Ex. **D♯**   **G♯**   **B♯**   **A♯**   **E♯**   **C♯**   **F♯**

3. In the blank, write the **sharp name** of the circled key on Merlin's robe.

Merlin's School

"A sharp can be on a line or in a space."

1. Draw several sharps on the line below. ✎   Draw several sharps in the space below. ✎

Hint: The line passes through the middle of the sharp.

Hint: The sharp "boxes in" the space.

"A sharp carries through an entire measure but not past a bar line."

2. How many notes are played as **F sharp**? _____

How many notes are played as **C sharp**? _____

How many notes are played as **G sharp**? _____

"The sharp sign is always written in front of the note."

3. Draw a sharp **in front of** each note below. Write the note name inside Merlin's hat.

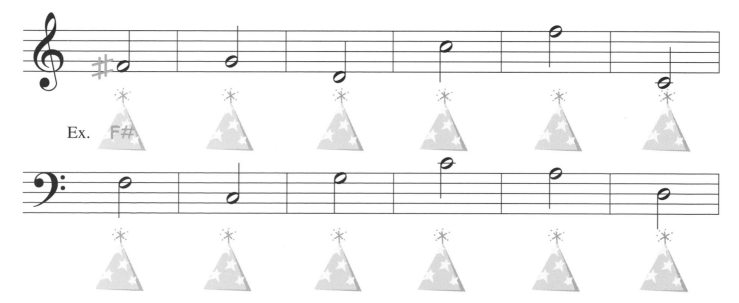

Ex. F#

The Flat ♭

A *flat* means to play the key a **half step lower** (the closest key to the left).

Party Game with Flats

1. Trace these flats.

Now draw a flat in each party hat.

2. Connect each **flat letter name** to the correct key on the keyboard.

D♭   G♭   B♭   E♭   A♭   C♭   F♭

3. Draw a flat **in front** of each note. Then name the note.

A flat can be on a line or space.

On the staff, a flat is always written **in front** of the note.

Ex. __E♭__ ____ ____ ____ ____ ____

Broadway Tunes

Sightread the examples below.
Watch carefully for sharps and flats!

a. *mf* Broad - way! Here we come. Broad - way! Mu - sic fun.

b. *mf* Broad - way danc - in'! Peo - ple danc - in' on the stage.

c. *mp* Come and see the cit - y lights. Watch the Broad-way show to-night.

Your teacher will play two notes for each example.
The second note will be a half step higher or lower than the first note.

- Draw a ♯ **in front of** the second note if it is **higher.**
- Draw a ♭ **in front of** the second note if it is **lower.**

LISTEN...

1. 2. 3.

4. 5. 6.

7. 8. 9.

Note to Teacher: In each of the above examples, **sharp** or **flat** the *second* note.

Tonic and Dominant Notes

In the C 5-finger scale and other 5-finger scales that you will learn:

The first note
is called the
tonic.

The fifth note
is called the
dominant.

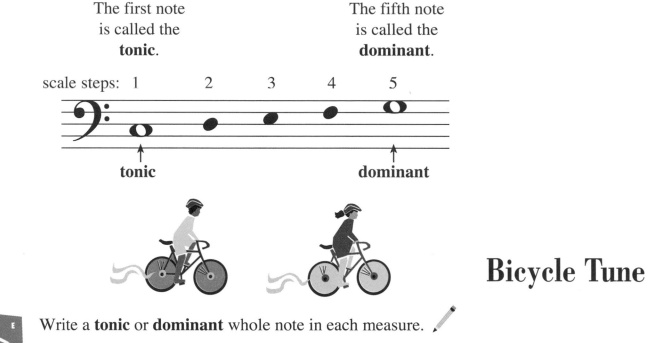

Bicycle Tune

Write a **tonic** or **dominant** whole note in each measure.

- If the melody is mostly scale steps 1-3-5, use the **tonic**.
- If the melody is mostly scale steps 2-4-5, use the **dominant**.

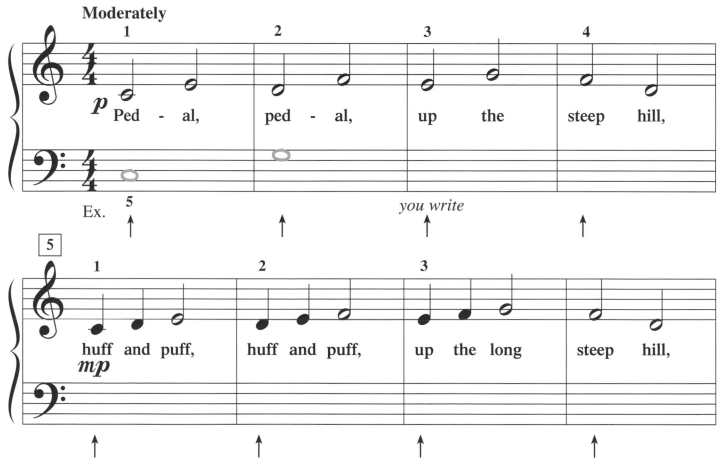

Moderately

Ped - al,   ped - al,   up   the   steep   hill,

you write

Ex.

huff and puff,   huff and puff,   up   the   long   steep   hill,

9

Just a lit - tle | far - ther now, | I'll be at the | top!

mf

13

s-l-o-w-i-n-g down

f Com - ing down, I'm | com - ing down, I'm | brak - ing to a | stop!

- Play your completed *Bicycle Tune*. You have **harmonized** the melody!

 Your teacher will play a short example that will end on the **tonic** or **dominant**. Circle the bicycle wheel with the correct answer. (Each example begins on the tonic.)

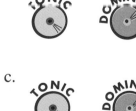

a.   TONIC   DOMINANT

b.   TONIC   DOMINANT

c.   TONIC   DOMINANT

d.   TONIC   DOMINANT

For Teacher Use Only: The examples may be played in any order.
Create more examples of your own for the student to verbally answer.

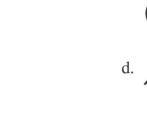

The C Chord

The C chord builds UP
in **3rds** (thirds) from C.

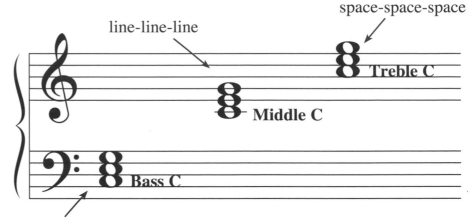

line-line-line

space-space-space

Treble C

Middle C

Bass C

space-space-space

Chords for a Scarecrow

1. Write a **C chord** starting on each C below.
   Hint: Refer to the chords above for help.

Bass C

Middle C

Treble C

Chords in the Cornfield

2. Add the missing notes *up* or *down* to form C chords.
   Remember, **C should be the bottom note of the chord**.

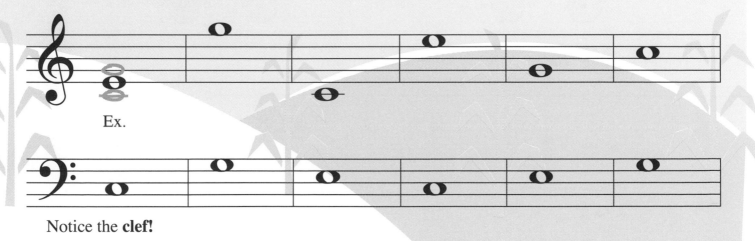

Ex.

Notice the **clef!**

I is the
Roman numeral
for the number **1**.

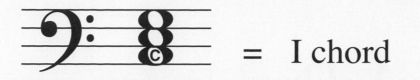 = **I chord**

In the C 5-finger scale, the C chord is called the **I chord** because it builds up from scale step 1.

Row, Row, Row Your Chords

Circle each C chord, then write a **I** (Roman numeral) underneath. Remember, C should be the *bottom* note of each C chord.

Draw an X through the other chords.

Ex. **I**

Notice the **clef!**

Your teacher will play either example **a** or **b**. Listen carefully and circle the one you hear.

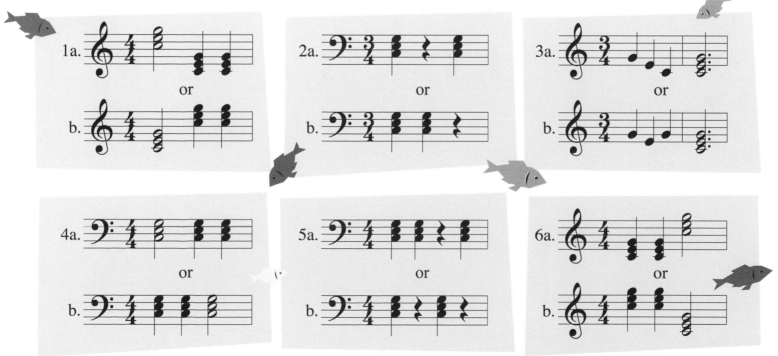

The V⁷ Chord

(pronounced "five-seven")

V is the Roman numeral for the number **5**.

The V⁷ chord is formed by playing both the dominant note and
the note below it in the 5-finger scale.

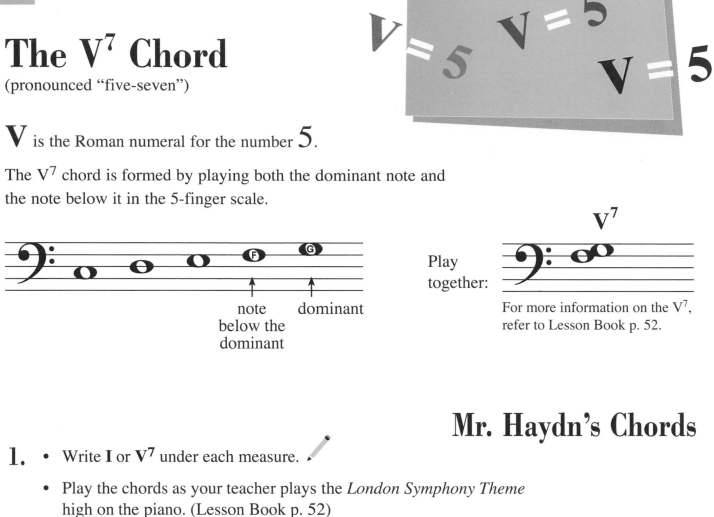

note
below the
dominant   dominant

Play
together:

V⁷

For more information on the V⁷,
refer to Lesson Book p. 52.

Mr. Haydn's Chords

1. • Write **I** or **V⁷** under each measure. ✎

• Play the chords as your teacher plays the *London Symphony Theme*
high on the piano. (Lesson Book p. 52)

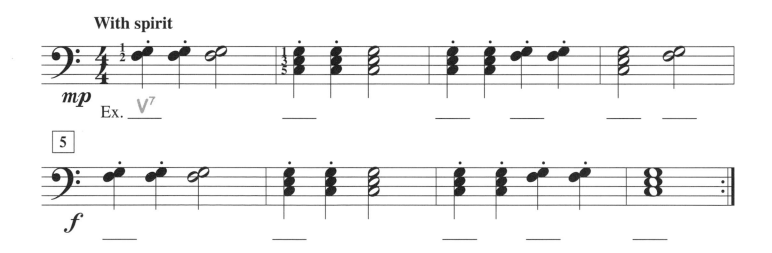

With spirit

mp Ex. __V⁷__   ____   ____ ____ ____ ____

5

f ____   ____   ____ ____ ____

2. Write **I** or **V⁷** in each of Mr. Haydn's wigs. Now play the chord pattern you wrote. ✎

Fun Facts for Mr. Haydn

1. Read the words, then play each melody.

2. Now write **I** or **V⁷** in each box to harmonize the melody.

   - If the R.H. plays mostly scale steps 1-3-5, use the **I** chord.
   - If the R.H. plays mostly scale steps 2-4-5, use the **V⁷** chord.

3. Play each melody with the chords.

Ex. ☐ I ☐ ☐ ☐

f-p Hay-dn was the sec-ond child of twelve chil-dren.
Hay-dn's fa-ther worked as a wag-on mak-er.

☐ ☐ ☐ ☐

f-p Aus-tri-a was Hay-dn's home, Hay-dn's home, Hay-dn's home.
As a child he loved to sing, loved to sing, loved to sing.

☐ ☐ ☐ ☐

f-p Hay-dn loved to hunt and Hay-dn was a fish-er-man.
Hay-dn thought of na-ture. Na-ture helped him to com-pose.

☐ ☐ ☐ ☐

f-p Guess how man-y sym-pho-nies that Hay-dn wrote?
Here's the an-swer: one hun-dred and four, he wrote!

- Your teacher will play each line of music and change the rhythm or notes of **one** measure.

- Look closely and point to the measure that was changed.

rit. = ritardando

means a gradual slowing down.

Ritardando is often shortened to *ritard.* or *rit.*

Fun Facts for Mr. Beethoven

1. Add **bar lines** to match the time signature.
Then sightread the music.

2. Now write **I** or **V⁷** in the boxes to harmonize each melody.
Play the melodies again with the chords.

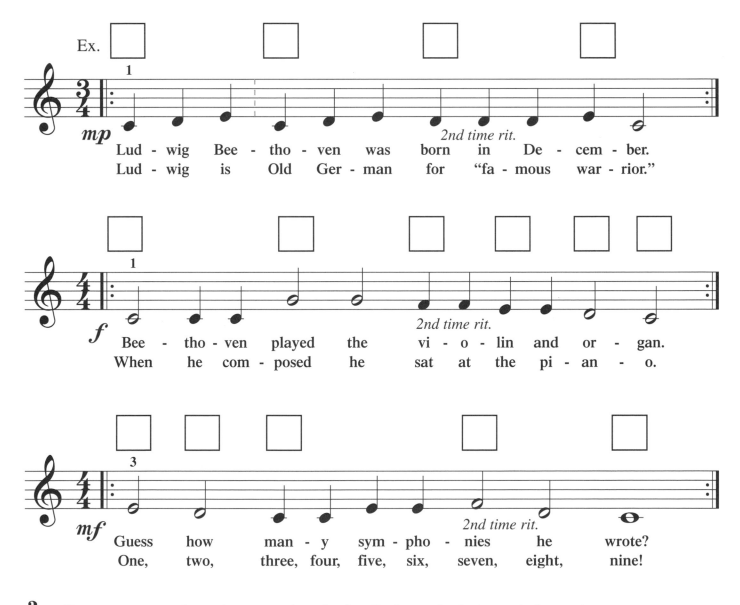

Ex.

$\frac{3}{4}$

mp

Lud - wig   Bee - tho - ven   was   born   in   De - cem - ber.
Lud - wig   is   Old   Ger - man   for   "fa - mous   war - rior."

2nd time rit.

$\frac{4}{4}$

f

Bee - tho - ven   played   the   vi - o - lin   and   or - gan.
When   he   com - posed   he   sat   at   the   pi - an - o.

2nd time rit.

$\frac{4}{4}$

mf

Guess   how   man - y   sym - pho - nies   he   wrote?
One,   two,   three, four,   five,   six,   seven,   eight,   nine!

2nd time rit.

3. Can you answer these three questions? Hint: Refer to the lyrics to help you!

Question:
What does the name
Ludwig mean?

Question:
Did Beethoven play
other instruments?

Question:
How many
symphonies did
Beethoven write?

An Eye for Chords

Sightread the music below. Set a steady beat and keep your eyes moving ahead.

Cheerfully

a.

mp 1 3 5   1 2

5 *broken chord*

rit.

Like a march

b.

mf 1 3 5   *rest!*   1 2

5

1. Put your L.H. in the **Bass C 5-finger scale**.

2. Close your eyes as your teacher plays a short example using **I** and **V⁷** chords.

3. Listen and play back what you hear.

Note: If two pianos are available, the teacher and student can each play in the same octave.

For Teacher Use Only: The teacher may play the examples in any order.

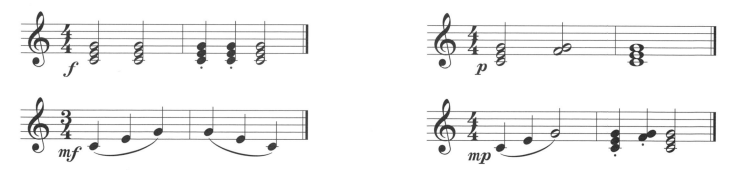

It is recommended that teachers continue by creating patterns of their own.

Three G's on the Grand Staff

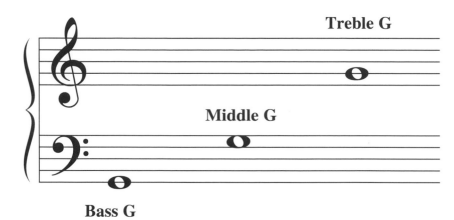

Treble G

Middle G

Bass G

Bongo Drums Play G's

1. Draw a **whole note** on the correct G for each drum.

This G has a low,
bass sound.

This G is a 5th
ABOVE Bass C.

This G is a 5th
ABOVE Middle C.

This G is an octave
ABOVE Bass G.

This G is known as
Treble G.

This G is known as
Bass G.

2. Your teacher will point to a drum above. Play that G on the piano.

G 5-Finger Scales on the Grand Staff

Chord Guy Is the Leader!

• Complete Chord Guy's instructions for each example.

Write a G 5-finger scale up from **Bass G**.

Write a G 5-finger scale up from **Treble G**.

Name these **intervals**.

Write **I** or **V⁷** in each box.

Hint: Look for broken chords, too!

In the G scale, name the **tonic** and **dominant** notes.

tonic

dominant

accent mark

> or > means accent the note by playing it **louder** than the others around it.

Dinosaur Tails Thump Accents!

1. Draw an accent mark **under beat 1** of each measure. Then play. ✎

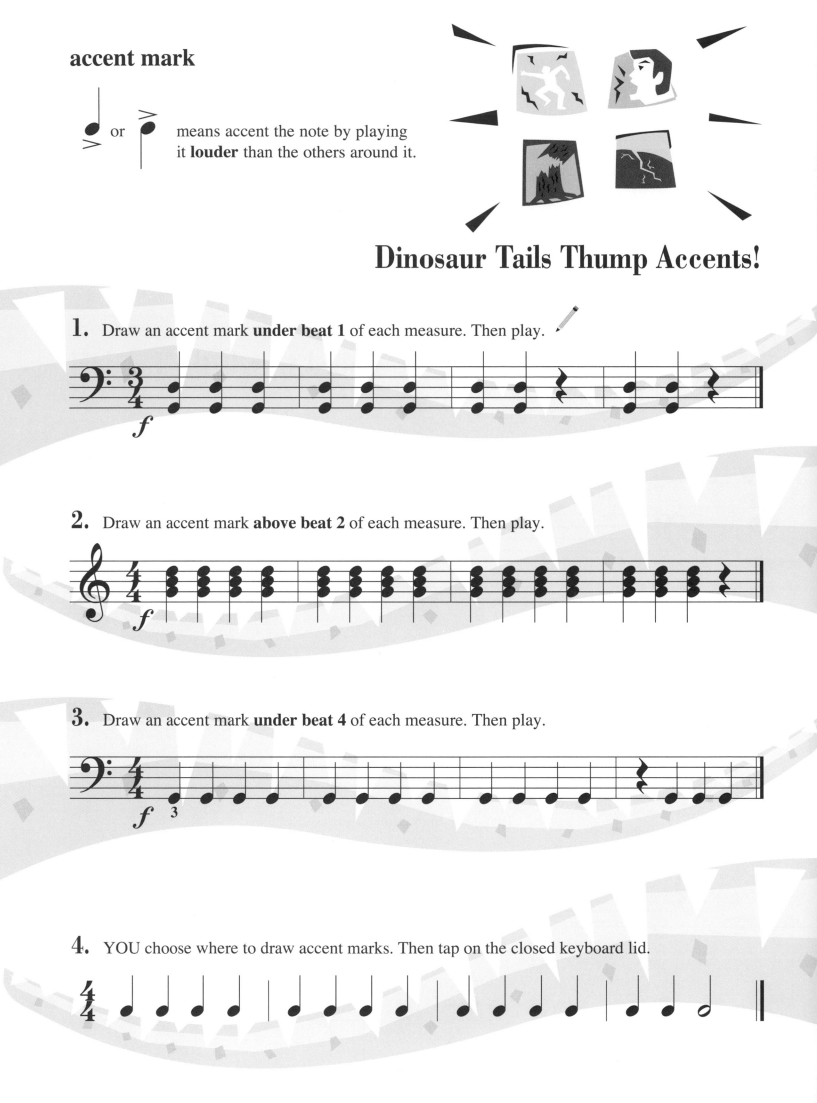

2. Draw an accent mark **above beat 2** of each measure. Then play.

3. Draw an accent mark **under beat 4** of each measure. Then play.

4. YOU choose where to draw accent marks. Then tap on the closed keyboard lid.

Dinosaur Dance Improv

Improvise "dinosaur dance" by doing the following:

- First, listen to your teacher play the accompaniment. Feel the strong dance beat.

- When you are ready, play notes IN ANY ORDER from a high **G 5-finger scale**. Listen! When your teacher plays softly, can you play softly? Match your teacher's dynamics.

- To end, play a final G.

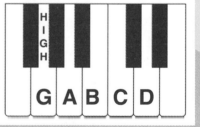

D
C
B
A
G

5
1
4
2
3
3
2
4

R.H. 1
or
L.H. 5

Play on a
HIGH G scale.

Teacher Improv Accompaniment

🎵 Lesson p.58 (Dinosaur Stomp)

Castle of Toys

1. Collect a toy by completing the challenge that is in each "room."

2. Then circle the toy and follow the arrows through the castle.
Your goal is to arrive at the tower where you can go down the water slide!

Name the interval.

This upbeat begins on beat _____ ?

Draw a Bass C.

Draw a half rest to complete the measure.

Write the notes for the G 5-finger scale. (Use whole notes.)

Draw a G chord.

Draw a whole rest to complete the measure.

Draw a whole note up a 5th from G.

Draw two different whole note G's on the staff.

Draw a quarter rest to complete the measure.

Write in the letter names for the G 5-finger scale.

Enter here !

Write your initials here.
YOU MADE IT!

Each example has one or more **upbeats.**
Answer each question and then sightread the music.

P O P Tunes!

Begins on beat ___ ?

a.

It went   POP!   It went   POP!   Did you   hear my bub- ble   POP?

Begins on beat ___ ?

b.

I'll   blow   a   big   bub - ble   and   then watch it   POP!

Begins on beat ___ ?

c.

I blew   a   great   big   bub - ble,   then   it went   POP!

Your teacher will play two melodies for each example.
Circle **same** or **different**.

1. same   2. same   3. same

    differENT   differENT   differENT

4. same   5. same   6. same

    differENT   differENT   differENT

For Teacher Use Only: The examples may be played in any order. (Choose your own dynamics for each pair.)

Final Review (UNITS 1-10)

Trophy Time!

Connect each example on the left to the matching trophy on the right.

CDEFG

go up a half step

the tie

smooth and connected

2 beats of silence

go down a half step

whole rest

slow down

interval of a 3rd

slur

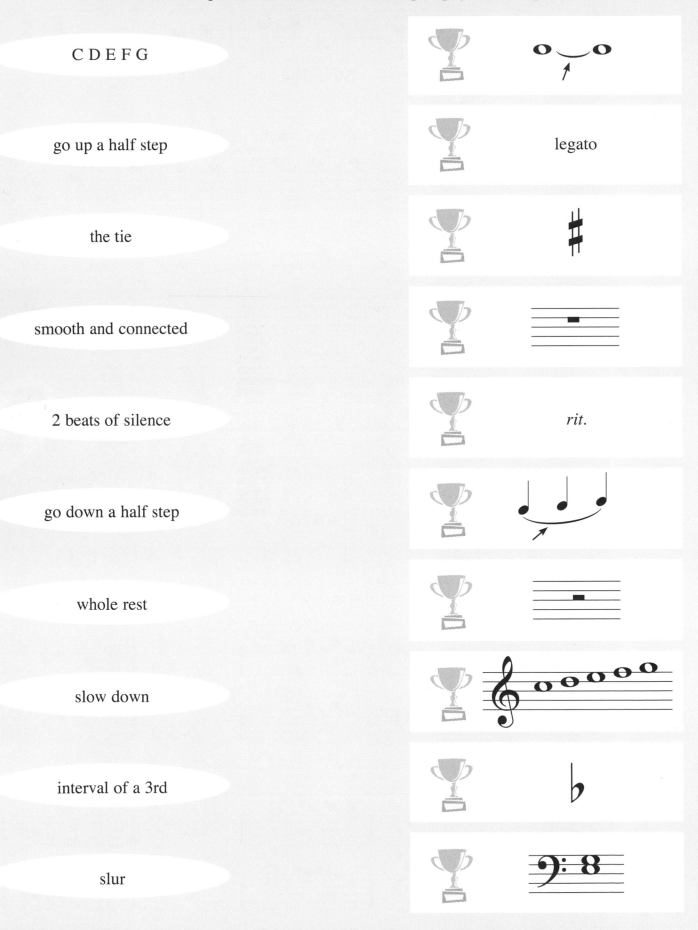